MW00526568

HELPING YOUR CHILDREN
Prayer Warriors

All rights reserved. No part of this book may be reproduced, stored in a retrieval system, or transmitted in any form by any means—electronic, mechanical, photocopy, recording or otherwise—without prior permission of the publisher, except as provided by U.S. copyright law.
© Future Flying Saucers, Anne Marie Gosnell

ISBN: 978-0-9981968-4-8, 978-0-9981968-5-5 (e-book)

Scripture quotations taken from the New American Standard Bible® (NASB), Copyright © 1960, 1962,
1963, 1968, 1971, 1972, 1973, 1975, 1977, 1995 by The Lockman Foundation. Used by permission.
www.Lockman.org

Publishing and design by: Stephanie Eidson, themultitaskinmom.com

Thank you for purchasing this book!

It is my prayer that the ideas and activities in this book will help your child begin, or continue, the spiritual discipline of prayer. You might find some fun helps for yourself as well!

For free Bible object lessons, visit futureflyingsaucers.com.

Be sure to join my Facebook group Bible Lessons for Kids for more fun, engaging Bible lessons and resources that can be used in the home or at church. We have a lot of fun in there, and I enjoy getting to know YOU better!

Many blessings,

Anne Marie Gosnell

Find my other books and resources online:

Walk This Way: Ethics and Sanctification Lessons for Kids

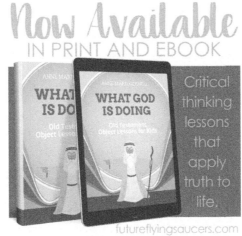

What God Is Doing: Old Testament Object Lessons for Kids

4

HELPING YOUR CHILDREN BECOME
PRAYER WARRIORS

ANNE MARIE GOSNELL

Table of Contents:

"Truly I say to you, unless you are converted and become like children, you will not enter the kingdom of heaven." ~ Jesus

Prayer.

How do you pray? Do you wake up early in the morning? Do you burn the midnight oil? Do you hide in the closet in the afternoon for five minutes of refreshing time with the Lord? Do you praise Him with song in the car? Do you get down on your knees, or stand and raise your hands?

Matthew 18:3 tells us to come to Jesus as little children. Think about that a minute. We adults are to come to God as a child would come to a parent.

When we pray, we are simply to come to Him as we are. Ourselves. Sinners. And we go to Him because of who He is.

We don't need to use big words. We don't need a loud and mighty voice that might reach heaven's door.

Lives change because of prayer. I've seen it. Perspectives change, attitudes change, hearts change . . .

<u>And the enemy knows the power of prayer.</u>

So just pray.

Do you want to improve your prayer time?

Pray.

Go to Him. He loves you and really does care about what is going on in your life.

He rejoices over you and each moment you give to Him.

Walk boldly to the throne; kneel and talk to your Father who loves you.

Then wait. Meditate on scripture. Listen to the inner presence of the Holy Spirit.

Then obey the still, small Voice.

Prayer allows us to be the channel through which God works. I want to teach prayer concepts to my children, but I have to grow in prayer myself and allow them to see my journey. I need to share with them what God tells me. I need to serve with sacrifice and praise.

It is through our example that our children will learn to pray.

In this book are tips and ideas that will help you build your own prayer life as you teach your children how to pray.

At the back of the book are scripture cards that can be printed and used. I Choose one or two cards to use at a time. Tape the cards to the wall by your child's bed, or on the mirror in the bathroom. Have the scripture visible and accessible. Praying scripture is a wonderful way to memorize it.

I recommend that you start at the beginning and work your way through to the end. If it takes you a while to work through the book, that's OK.

The Bible tells us that God provides everything we need and that promise includes the protection and tools needed to develop a dynamic prayer life. One thing we can do to help our children be prepared to pray is to teach them about the Armor of God.

There is a song I used to teach my church kids called, "I'm in the Lord's Army". When we choose to live a life for Jesus we enter His army. We really do become "Christian Soldiers". Our battle is not with other people, but with the powers of darkness and our own weak flesh.

A soldier would never go into battle without body armor. That would be ludicrous, not to mention deadly. But we do it every day when we leave our beds and enter the day without putting on the armor of God.

We must be dressed each day. We teach our children how to dress themselves. We also need to teach them how to put on their spiritual dress for the day.

Working through this book yourself and with your children is a great beginning. In fact, it might be good to revisit the exercises in this book every few years as your children grow in Christ and are ready to add more weapons to their arsenal.

New habits take a while to form. Keep on keeping on!

I looked on Google, so it must be correct. Right? I found websites and blog posts that had resource after resource for:

- scriptures to pray for your kids;
- scriptures to pray over your kids; or
- popular kids' prayers to pray for your kids.

But I didn't find much to help parents teach their children how to use scripture to pray. (I did find a few resources that are foundational to teaching our kids to pray.)

There are formula prayers. Bedtime prayers. Memorized prayers. Mealtime prayers. There are acronym prayer methods such as ACTS and PRAY.

I am not going to say that those prayers are wrong. I grew up speaking some of those prayers and formulas myself. But here again, these make a great foundation for a powerful prayer life.

Jesus had a great prayer life. After all, He was so used to talking with His Father on a regular basis that He drew near to Him whenever He had a chance. When Jesus taught the disciples the Lord's Prayer, He showed how intimate our conversations could be. When Jesus was tempted in the desert, He showed us how scripture is powerful against the enemy. When Jesus was mocked and accused of blasphemy, He used scripture to prove how He fulfilled the law.

The more I learn about Jesus, the more I learn how to talk with Him. In watching Jesus' example, I have learned that when I pray, I need to speak His words back to Him. Praying scripture is not for the Lord's benefit, but for ours. **If we are able to articulate the meaning of the scripture, then we understand what God is trying to teach us.** Sometimes it takes praying a scripture and talking it out with Jesus to truly understand what it means and how it applies to my life.

Praying scripture helps us to memorize that scripture. Then the Holy Spirit can add that Truth to His arsenal when we need it to fight the enemy.

I want that for my children. I want them to pray scripture to their Lord. But that takes time and practice.

How to Teach children to Turn Scripture into Prayers

1. **Change the pronouns.** If the scripture includes we or me or they or us, change the pronoun to fit the situation. For example, look at 2 Timothy 1:7.

> *"For God has not given us a spirit of timidity, but of power and love and discipline."*

Now, change the us to me and see how powerful that prayer becomes. To make it even more powerful, change the word God to You, because we're speaking to God. Try it!

> *"For [You have] not given [me] a spirit of timidity, but of power and love and discipline."*

Whew! Imagine how great a prayer like this could be for a little one who needs to face some fears, or wants to tackle some self-discipline issues.

2. **Include names of people.** This one is a little harder grammatically to explain. If a scripture has a direct object or another similar word, replace it with a person's name. For example, look at John 3:16.

> *"For God so loved the world, that He gave His only begotten Son, that whoever believes in Him shall not perish, but have eternal life."*

Change the world to [your name], and whoever to when [your name]. Then insert he or she before shall. This personalizes the gospel, and kids LOVE it!! Try it!

> *"For God so loved [your name], that He gave His only begotten Son, that [when (your name)] believes in Him [he/she] shall not perish, but have eternal life."*

God loves YOU. Look what He DID for you! That's pretty awesome.

3. **Try this scripture on your own.** See if you match mine! Proverbs 3:5-6

> *"Trust in the Lord with all your heart And do not lean on your own understanding. In all your ways acknowledge Him, And He will make your paths straight."*

Now pray the scripture.

Did you get something like this?

> *Lord, help me to trust in [You] with all [my] heart and [to] not lean on [my]*

own understanding. [May I] in all [my] ways acknowledge [You], and [You] will make [my] paths straight. ~ Amen!

Praying scripture becomes easier the more you do it. Practice with your kids. Have them help turn scriptures into prayers and write them down.

14

Although it might seem logical to us, not all people realize to whom they are praying when they begin a habit of prayer. It is important for our children to understand the *Who* and the *Why* of prayer.

To Whom Are We Praying?

Christians pray to God. The scriptures tell us that there is one God and that He created everything. No one created God, and God will never end. God is good. God is just. God is righteous. God is perfect.

Why Do We Pray?

In the Bible, God tells us to pray. Jesus, as an example to us, prayed to His Father.

People are sinful. We are not eternal. We are the created and will die one day. But we are eternal souls, and God wants us to forever be with Him. We must depend upon Him for salvation.

Because He created us, God wants a relationship with us. A relationship takes communication. God communicates to us through the Bible. It is God's Word. We can communicate back to God through prayer. So it makes sense for us to read God's words to us and then talk to Him about His Word and how we can apply it to our lives.

Praying and communicating with God allows us to know what God expects from us and what His plan is for our lives.

God Is Our Father.

When teaching our kids to pray, we need to show by example that God is a father figure. He provides, protects, and loves His children dearly. Some children do not have an earthly father, or a good example of a father, and so their image of a heavenly Father can be skewed.

The enemy does not want our kids to have a proper realization of God. The enemy does not want us to understand God's love and power.

In Matthew 6:9-13, Jesus exemplified prayer for us by praying to His Father. We need to do the same.

Prepare to Pray!

Use the scriptures in the back of this book to lead your child in prayer. If you have younger children, choose 1 or 2 verses to focus on. For older children, encourage them to choose a verse to memorize.

When a child disobeys, and you are displeased with them, the relationship you have with that child is harmed. When you have harmed someone else, you know that the relationship between you and that other person is broken in some manner.

But relationships with others can be fixed and healed. How? By apologizing for what we did and making restitution. We teach our kids to say, *"I'm sorry. Please forgive me. How can I make up for what I did to you?"* When you argue with a friend or spouse, you apologize and work at the relationship to heal what was broken.

When we sin, our relationship with God is harmed. When a person is aware of their sin and how it displeases God, then the desire to heal the relationship becomes urgent. No one wants the stress that comes with being at odds with another person. The same goes for being in strife with God.

Asking for forgiveness from God and others allows our hearts to be at peace. Knowing you are forgiven brings about a clean slate—a "do-over."

Does healing need to take place? Sure. Do we need to work at changing something about ourselves? Probably.

But asking for forgiveness is the first step. When our children realize that having a healthy relationship with God brings them peace of heart and mind, then we need to be ready to guide them into the beginnings of sanctification. When this humbleness begins, THAT is when the Holy Spirit can begin to take over and transform our children into images of Jesus.

Prepare to Pray!

Use the scriptures in the back of this book to lead your child in prayer. If you have younger children, choose 1 or 2 verses to focus on. For older children, encourage them to choose a verse to memorize.

When we pray, there are certain words or phrases that everyone knows to say. We've heard prayer modeled by others, and we copy what we hear. Most of the time we end with "Amen," because we are to be "in agreement" with whoever is praying. But why do we say, "In Jesus' Name?"

A good name is to be respected. A king can tell a servant to go do something "in the name of the king," and it will be done and accepted. No questions asked.

In the Old Testament, God tells us to not take His name in vain. There is a meaning in a "great name" that Americans do not truly understand.

Use God's Name for Good.

In Matthew 18:5, Jesus tells us, *"And whoever receives one such child in My name receives Me."* When we say we are Christians, which means "little Christ," we are taking Jesus' name upon ourselves. When we do kind acts of service, then we are using His name for good.

Be Respectful of God's Name.

We must be respectful of God's name. After all, He is the Creator of the universe. Many verses of scripture link together God's name with power.

"Nevertheless He saved them for the sake of His name, That He might make His power known." ~ Psalm 106:8

When we pray, we must be respectful toward the One to whom we are praying. **When we ask for help, guidance, or salvation, we are wanting heaven to move on our behalf.** That thought alone should humble our hearts.

Use Jesus' Name Against the Enemy.

"These signs will accompany those who have believed: in My name they will cast out demons, they will speak with new tongues . . ." ~ Mark 16:17

"The seventy returned with joy, saying, 'Lord, even the demons are subject to us in Your name.'" ~ Luke 10:17

Our fight is never with each other. Our fight is against the prince of darkness and the principalities of the air. Once again this shows the power of praying in the name of Jesus. His name is the only one that can bind the enemy and save us from destruction.

So Why Do We Pray in Jesus' Name?

We pray in Jesus' name because of John 14:13: *"Whatever you ask in My name, that will I do, so that the Father may be glorified in the Son."*

We can also add John 14:26 and John 15:16. These words come from Jesus, and He meant them.

Prepare to Pray!

Have your children think about former prayers they may have said. Explain to them the concept of being a "little Christ" and remind them that there is great power in the name of Jesus. Remind them that we humbly go before the Father to pray because He is great and mighty. We are not. Tell your children that when they end their prayers with the phrase, "In Jesus' name," then they are to expect Him to answer. If they need to deal with sin or pray against the enemy, help your children to claim, "In Jesus' name."

Children need to know that it is OK to talk to God whenever and wherever they are. Young kids can be literal, and they may think that they can only pray when at church or at the dinner table. Older kids might think that they must be alone in order to pray to God.

We must communicate that God is ready to listen to prayers anytime and anywhere. Whether the child is alone or in a crowd; speaks silently or out loud; speaks a short prayer or one that takes a while; each must understand that she is heard and has direct access to God.

Morning

God's mercies are new every morning. Wouldn't the Lord love it if we woke up saying, "Good morning, Jesus!" At some point during the morning, be sure to gather everyone together and pray for the day. Ask for God's peace to dwell in everyone's hearts as they go throughout the day, and lift up any known needs.

If you have littles whom you still dress, consider talking about the armor of God as you help them put on each item of clothing: pants, shoes, belt, hat, etc. This is a great way to begin the habit of putting on the whole armor of God each day.

Meals

Matthew 14:19 shows Jesus blessing the food before handing it out. We should do the same thing. Food gives our bodies health and life. God cares about our lives, and He's the one who provides the food. Saying mealtime prayers is a great way for your children to practice praying aloud.

While I don't think you need to use the same mealtime prayer every meal, I do think you can use scripture to help create meaningful blessings. Choosing parts of Psalm 104 is a great start. You could also lead your family to sing the doxology.

Leaving Home and Coming Home

"And thus you shall say, 'Have a long life, peace be to you, and peace be to your house, and peace be to all that you have.'" ~ 1 Samuel 25:6

Always strive for peace in your home. Teach forgiveness and patience. You want your house to be a safe haven for your children. You want them to be sad to leave and happy to come home.

When leaving for an extended amount of time, pray as a family that God will guard your home. He provided everything and, yes, He could take it away. But you can pray to the One who gave it and thank Him for the blessings that are held inside the walls of your home.

When you return, thank the Lord for blessing you with a home in which to return.

Bedtime

The best conversations you will ever have with your children will probably come at bedtime. This is when they tell you about their burdens, hopes, feelings, uncertainties, and questions. Bedtime routine takes almost an hour at our home with three children. There are days when it can be burdensome in and of itself. **But I know that what my husband and I are doing in these first years of life with our kids will be foundational for their prayer lives in the future.**

Lead your children in prayer. Pray using some of the strategies from this book. Pray for good thoughts and good dreams. Make bedtime prayers a habit, and tell Jesus, "Good Night!"

Maybe There Are More Times to Pray?

"These words, which I am commanding you today, shall be on your heart. You shall teach them diligently to your sons and shall talk of them when you sit in your house and when you walk by the way and when you lie down and when you rise up." ~ Deuteronomy 6:6-7

"Pray without ceasing." ~ 1 Thessalonians 5:17

Model prayer during bad times and good times, in times of urgency, when you are discouraged, and . . . ALL the time.

Prepare to Pray!

To help you begin the process of praying continually, try this exercise with your children. The next time you hear a siren or see emergency lights, particularly those of an ambulance or a fire engine, stop what you and the children are doing and pray. Pray for the person who might be hurt. Pray for the paramedics as they help the person. Pray for the firemen, that God might keep them safe. Once you model this a few times, you will find that your children will jump at the chance to pray.

Friends with cancer. Family members needing healing or dying. Natural disasters. Personal life decisions. Injury. How does our faith handle such large prayers? What about our children? How can we teach them to pray about big things?

If we teach our kids to pray for big, hard situations and the outcome doesn't match the desire, won't the faith of our kids be shaken? Should we even bother to pray?

It is our job to pray to the Lord and then accept the outcomes in faith. God has certain plans for us, and we must rely on the truth that God is wiser than we are. Does this mean we must be happy when bad things happen to us or when prayer situations don't end the way we want them to?

No. In fact, God is big enough to accept our weeping, our questions, and our emotions. But we are to pray anyway. **Our part of prayer communication is to listen and ask. God's part is to listen and act in everyone's best interest.**

Our children need to know that nothing is too big for God. He is still a God of miracles. God raised Jesus from the dead. That is power! The same power that raised Jesus from the dead is the power of the Holy Spirit who dwells inside of each believer.

Sometimes children have needs that seen little to us, but those needs are important to your children and important to God. It is easy for a parent to dismiss something that we consider a little worry, but it might be a HUGE worry to the child.

Teach your kids to pray . . . no matter what. And you never know. The faith of your child might strengthen your own faith.

Prepare to Pray!

Use the scriptures in the back of this book to lead your child in prayer. If you have younger children, choose 1 or 2 verses to focus on. For older children, encourage them to choose a verse to memorize.

"Ask, and it will be given to you; seek, and you will find; knock, and it will be opened to you." ~ Luke 9:11

Many times people turn to God like He is a Santa Claus. We have a long list of things we'd like from Him, and we ask them one by one, hoping that God will say yes to our prayers.

But God isn't Santa, nor do we want Him to be Santa. God is much bigger. He knows the whole context of our lives from beginning to end. Not only does He know what is best for us, but God is also our greatest cheerleader. **He's on our side and He wants to see us succeed in bringing Him glory.**

Our wants and desires might differ from God's wants and desires for us. He has many promises in scripture for us. **He has plans that do not harm us, but that transform us into the image of Jesus.**

God loves joy. Happiness is an emotion. It is temporary. Joy is of the Holy Spirit and is eternal.

When we teach our kids how to pray, we must verbalize that we can ask God for anything. **But it's the requests that fall in line with His plan to which He will say YES.**

Prayers to Which God Says Yes

The Bible is full of promises. If God has promised to do something, and we pray for Him to do it, then He has already promised that He will. For example, if we have done something wrong, and we are truly sorry and repent, then 1 John 1:9 promises us this: *"If we confess our sins, He is faithful and righteous to forgive us our sins and to cleanse us from all unrighteousness."* The Bible doesn't say maybe, or that God will think about it. No. He IS faithful to forgive if we confess.

Let's teach our kids to pray God's promises. He has promises about salvation, forgiveness, guidance from the Holy Spirit, finances, wisdom, healing, needs, protection, fears, family, marriage, parenting, overcoming temptation, and the end of suffering.

Prepare to Pray!

If your child is struggling with any of the topics listed, then find the promises about that topic in scripture. God has already said yes to some questions and prayers. For a great list of scriptures by topic, go to http://www.bibleinfo.com/en/topics/bible-promises

The greatest prayer we can ever pray is the one for eternal life, both for ourselves and those who are lost. God promises to give eternal life to those who believe and ask in Jesus' name.

When God Says "Not Now" to Our Prayers

"There is an appointed time for everything. And there is a time for every event under heaven..." ~ Ecclesiastes 3:1

Sometimes God answers prayers with, "Yes." Sometimes He answers, "No." But it's the "Not now" answers that can frustrate us. How should we help our kids understand God when He tells them, "Not now?"

There are two words our children need to understand. Those words are **appointed time**. Use the activity and verses in the back to help your child learn that God has a time for everything.

When God Says "Not Now" Prayer Activity

Materials: beans, a clear plastic cup, and a paper towel (You will want soil later when the plant is ready for it.)

Lesson: Because God is eternal, He knows what will happen in our lives. And because God has a good plan for us, He knows what He wants to do with our lives. When we pray and ask things of God, if those things are based on God's promises, then He will say "Yes". However, that "Yes" may not take place *when* we want it to.

In everything there is a season. The book of Ecclesiastes tells us that. There is a time to be joyful, and a time to be sad. There is a time for war, and a time for peace, etc. When God tells us "not now," it is usually because 1) He has something better for us in the present, or 2) the timing isn't right. It isn't the **appointed time** yet. Perhaps we need to grow more spiritually or mentally before a certain prayer is answered. No matter the reason, we can trust that God knows what is best for us.

Activity: Dampen the paper towel and place it inside the cup. Place three or four beans around the side of the cup so your child can watch the growth.

Ask: *We have now planted these beans. Will it take a short time or a long time for our plant to produce new bean pods?* (A long time)

Can the new pods form while the beans are in the cup like this? If not, why? (No, the plant is not ready to produce new bean pods yet.)

Prepare to Pray!

Pray with your child. Ask God, in His timing, to produce new beans. As you watch the plant grow, pray for new beans. When the time is right, transfer the beans into a pot with soil and continue to pray for new beans. When the new beans appear, thank God for His timing.

"Not now" answers to prayer usually teach us patience and grow our faith. Our job is to keep asking, seeking, trusting, and following the One who knows what is best for us.

You can relate asking God for things through prayer to how your child asks you for things. Think about the following example questions and answers and have a conversation about prayer requests.

Mom, can I have a pet elephant? *No, we do not have room, nor would it be happy here.*

Mom, can I read a book? *No, it's about time to go to bed.*

Mom, can I read a book? *Yes! Please do and we can read together.*

God, can I have a million dollars? *No, you are being selfish.*

God, can I have a million dollars? *No, it would corrupt you.*

God, can I have a million dollars? *No, I am building you up through struggle.*

God, can I have exactly what I need so that I can do what you have told me to do? *Yes! And let's do this together.*

"Now He was telling them a parable to show that at all times they ought to pray and not to lose heart." ~ Luke 18:1

Ballgames, dentist and doctor appointments, recitals or concerts, hospital visits, oral reports . . .

Our children are involved in many different activities and events. If your calendar is like mine, the boxes become filled quickly.

Nobody likes to endure pain or discomfort. Sometimes kids have to endure broken bones or face an audience that awaits their talents. Nerves jump and butterflies flitter in their stomachs.

What about fear of the unknown? Is it possible your child might be facing the filling of a cavity? Or maybe you are awaiting even harder news, such as dealing with a disease.

Perhaps your child doubts his/her ability to catch the ball or sing a solo? You know God has gifted them with amazing abilities, but maybe they don't have confidence yet.

You can help your child pray about events on the calendar. Help them place their trust in the God who gave them gifts and abilities, and who provides them with everything they need.

How to Pray Before an Event

Before an event, ask your child how he is feeling. You know your child. You know whether or not he will need to deal with sportsman-like attitudes or doubts.

Help your child to pray for:

1. God to be glorified through all words and actions (1 Peter 4:11)

2. The ability to do well (1 Kings 2:3)

3. The others involved in the event (James 5:16)

4. The ability to remember what Jesus told us (John 14:26)

5. Safety (Psalm 91)

6. Confidence (Hebrews 10:34-36)

7. Graciousness in doing well, or when failure happens (Colossians 4:6)

Prepare to Pray!

Sometimes in the midst of an event, our kids become anxious. Teach your kids to pray one word: "Jesus." When the crazies are going on—Jesus. When pain hurts—Jesus. When about to walk on stage—Jesus.

He's all they need.

"And he answered, 'I will not'; but afterward he regretted it and went." ~ Matthew 21:29

"Remind them to be subject to rulers, to authorities, to be obedient, to be ready for every good deed, to malign no one, to be peaceable, gentle, showing every consideration for all men." ~ Titus 3:1-2

If we're really honest with ourselves, we probably don't like that verse in Titus. And from day one, our kids have that same sin nature. Jesus knows this, which is why He told us the parable of the prodigal son. All of us have disobeyed, but through repentance, we turn back to the One who loves us unconditionally.

The more God forgives me, the more I desire to obey Him. **Sin seems more awful the more you deal with it.** God must be the one who deals with the hearts of our children, but we can lead them to pray for the desire to obey Him and the authorities placed over them.

Who DID Have the Desire to Obey?

If you haven't already, introduce your children and students to Samuel. Samuel was human... although there are times when I wonder. (Just kidding!) The scriptures give us an amazing look into Samuel's life. We get to watch him grow up. We watch Samuel's mama praying for him. We watch her give Samuel over to Eli. And we watch how Samuel dealt with authority. Read 1 Samuel 3 with your children and discuss these questions:

1. What did Samuel hear in the night?

2. To whom did he run?

3. Did he listen to the advice given to him?

4. What was the result of Samuel listening to Eli?

5. What did the voice tell Samuel?

6. Did Samuel want to tell Eli what the Lord had told him?

7. Did he obey anyway?

8. What would you have done if you were Samuel?

Prepare to Pray!

Discuss with your child which requests they have a hard time obeying. Is it when they are asked to clean the bedroom? Or practice the piano? Or when a teacher says to stop talking? Or to turn in homework on time?

Write these difficulties in your child's prayer journal, or on a sticky note to stick to a prayer wall. Help your child to pray, asking the Lord to help them WANT to do whatever it is that they are resisting.

Do you have older children? Have them do this exercise, but add for them to pray for YOU. Ask them to pray that you would be a good parent to them and that you would not aggravate them. Have them pray for you that you might have wisdom in training them in righteousness.

"And Jesus kept increasing in wisdom and stature, and in favor with God and men."
~ Luke 2:52

As parents and teachers, we want our children and students to grow in knowledge. We desire for them to do well in school. We enjoy watching them develop their talents. Observing children who persevere even when the objectives are difficult brings a smile of satisfaction to our faces.

But what if your child is struggling? What if there is anxiety before a test? What if learning issues are huge mountains to climb? What if, no matter how much you throw the ball, the bat never makes contact?

2 Timothy 1:7 tells us that God gives us a spirit of discipline, a sound mind, and sound judgment. Be aware that knowledge is different from wisdom. Yes, we want our kids to learn to the best of their abilities, but wisdom is better. Discernment is better. We parents have to help our kids learn how to think like Jesus. **But wisdom begins with knowledge. And knowledge comes from fear of the Lord.**

That means we must surround our kids with a biblical worldview. Every decision and action our kids take will be based upon how they view the world.

Teach Them to Pray for Knowledge

The fear of the Lord is recognizing that He is God and we are not. It's that easy. He is the master; we are the bondservants. The sooner our kids learn that, the better. But they have to deal with sin as we do. **Once our children come to the knowledge of saving faith, then wisdom and discernment can grow.**

Help your child pray for:

1. the ability to concentrate;

2. help to reason things through;

3. good thoughts;

4. help for solving problems;

5. eyes to see God's truth in each circumstance;

6. sin to be revealed;

7. knowledge of who they are in Christ;

8. and knowledge when they do not know what to do.

Prepare to Pray!

Use the scriptures in the back of this book to lead your child in prayer. If you have younger children, choose 1 or 2 verses to focus on. For older children, encourage them to choose a verse to memorize.

"Now we know that whatever the Law says, it speaks to those who are under the Law, so that every mouth may be closed and all the world may become accountable to God." ~ Romans 3:19

"Mama? When will the Twin Towers fall again?" my four-year-old asked.

TV. Radio. Computers. Phones. iPads. Kindles. The world is at the fingertips of our kids. The world is a scary place.

But it doesn't have to be. Christians know that God is still in charge no matter how bleak and dark the events of the world look. When our children hear something scary, or must be told some troubling news, don't skim over the situation.

Take it to God in prayer.

Channel the concerns of your children into prayer. Use troubling times to show how we should turn to the Lord first.

For example: Another terrorist explosion has taken place in Europe and some people have died. Ask: What would Jesus desire through this situation?

1. Jesus would want people to be healed if hurt because He is merciful.

2. He would want those who did wrong to be caught so they do not hurt people again because He is just.

3. Jesus would want salvation for all people involved in the event because that is why He came to earth in the first place.

Prayers like this allow our kids to take their focus off of fears and place it onto the One who can do all things. Let's teach our children that they are not helpless when facing world events. No. On the contrary, **they are powerful and productive when they turn to prayer.**

Prepare to Pray!

Think about fears your child exhibits or situations that have happened recently which seem to concern her. Use the scriptures in the back of this book to lead your child in prayer. If you have younger children, choose 1 or 2 verses to focus on. For older children, encourage them to choose a verse to memorize.

Teaching Children to Pray for Needy People

"The King will answer and say to them, 'Truly I say to you, to the extent that you did it to one of these brothers of Mine, even the least of them, you did it to Me.'" ~ Matthew 25:40

Needy people don't just come in the form of the homeless man or woman sitting on the corner these days. Sometimes the needy person is the child who was dropped off at school at 6 a.m. without breakfast and wearing shoes one size too large. Sometimes the needy person lives in the huge house on the corner which he and his wife bought back in the day and which is now about to be repossessed by the bank. Sometimes the needy person walks right past you, needing only a friendly smile, and you choose to look away instead.

Do needy people need our prayers? Absolutely! But this is where the rubber meets the road. This is when faith becomes tangible. This is when kids can watch God work through them to help others.

Teaching children to pray for needy people helps to build a compassionate attitude towards others. When your kids see a person in need, help them to pray for the needs to be met: shelter, food, provisions, medicine, and material needs. Then discuss what types of things you and your child might be able to do to help, if not that specific person, then someone else.

Prepare to Pray!

Choose one of the following activities to do with your child or students from the list found at :
https://www.futureflyingsaucers.com/teaching-kids-pray-needy-people-prayer-activity

As you work though the activity, or before you drop something off, use one or two of the verses listed at the back of this book to pray over the action you are doing and for the person who will be on the receiving end.

If none of those activities will work for you, try one of these:

1. Have your kids go through their toys and closet and find five items to give to a local charity.

2. Create a gift bag for the homeless.

3. Fill a backpack with school supplies and drop it off at your local public school. Tell the secretary to give it to a child in need.

Prepare to Pray!

Use the scriptures in the back of this book to lead your child in prayer. If you have younger children, choose 1 or 2 verses to focus on. For older children, encourage them to choose a verse to memorize.

If you noticed some of those verses . . . sometimes helping others is more about our own heart change. Encourage your children to not just read the words, but to pray them.

Teaching Children to Pray for Family

"These all with one mind were continually devoting themselves to prayer, along with the women, and Mary the mother of Jesus, and with His brothers." ~ Acts 1:14

Brothers, sisters, mom, dad, grandmothers, grandfathers, aunts, uncles, cousins . . . FAMILY! Many times those who are closest to us are the ones who are forgotten when it is time to pray.

We need to teach our children to pray for family. I don't know if your home is anything like mine, but my kids love to pick on and squabble with each other. Most of the time it is harmless and fun, but other times it turns into all-out war. Voices are raised, objects are thrown, and tears run down faces.

{Before you think I'm a bad mom for allowing such behavior, please know that there are discipline proceedings that take place when such actions are shown!}

I'm finding that in order to build harmony among my children, I need to lead them in praying for each other. And not only should they pray for each other, but for extended family as well.

Our children can pray for:

1. Good health and safety of family members *by name*.

2. US! Ask your kids to pray for you.

3. Specific problems other family members might be facing: exams, first day of high school, driving test, performance, job situation, etc.

In the process of teaching your children to pray for family members, you will become more active in the lives of the family as well. Ask for prayer updates and share those with your children. When a prayer has been answered, lead your children to pray and thank the Lord for His care. Help them to praise God when He does a gracious deed.

Prepare to Pray!

Have your children each get a sheet of paper and write down every family member's name on it. Help them to write one request for each person. If you aren't sure how to pray for someone, have your child ask him how you as a family can pray for him.

Once those are written down, have each child find a place to tape their list to the wall so it will be regularly seen. Sometimes the best place to put prayer lists is on the bathroom mirror!

Encourage your children to pray for two or three people each time they see the list. **And be sure to pray as a family.** Try to pray as a family four or five times per week.

"You are my hiding place; You preserve me from trouble; You surround me with songs of deliverance." ~ Psalm 32:7

God is always changing things. He is always up to something new. If we hang around Him long enough, then we are caught up in the excitement as we watch God do amazing things in and through us. But children are just beginning their journey with Jesus. Change can be scary.

But then again, I'm an adult . . . change can still be scary.

As we walk and talk with Jesus, we need to remember the truth found in Romans 8:28:

"And we know that God causes all things to work together for good to those who love God, to those who are called according to His purpose."

No matter the situation in which our children find themselves, the situation will eventually change, and it will be for their good. However, it sure would be good to pray about it in the midst of the event.

Prayer Changes Things: Deliverance!

Is your child facing a difficult friendship at school? Is someone being mean? Maybe a really hard exam is coming up? Maybe a bad decision was made? Perhaps there is an evil situation going on in your local community which concerns you? Pray for deliverance and changed hearts.

Prayer Changes Things: Courage!

When wickedness does present itself before our children—and it will—we want them armed and ready for battle! Just as Joseph had the courage to run from the evil of Potiphar's wife, we want our children to have the courage to flee from temptation and poor choices. Pray for courage and strong, righteous hearts.

Prepare to Pray!

Use the scriptures in the back of this book to lead your child in prayer. If you have younger children, choose 1 or 2 verses to focus on. For older children, encourage them to choose a verse to memorize.

42

When a person is kind to us or gives us something, the first thing we should want to do is speak thanks to them.

Interacting with God is no different.

God gives us many blessings every day. The first thing we should want to do is tell Him, "Thank you."

Thanksgiving Activity

Materials: journal or notebook, or scraps of paper and a large jar

Many times, we forget to be thankful because we do not pay attention to the blessings we receive.

Encourage your child to write down one blessing each day. Write the blessings as a list in a journal or notebook; OR write each blessing on a scrap of paper and put it in a Blessing Jar.

Do this for one month.

On the last day of the month, read through all of the blessings and discuss why your child should be thankful for those blessings.

Then have your child practice praying a prayer of thanksgiving to the Lord.

Prepare to Pray!

Use the scriptures in the back of this book to lead your child in prayer. If you have younger children, choose 1 or 2 verses to focus on. For older children, encourage them to choose a verse to memorize.

"I am weary with my sighing; Every night I make my bed swim, I dissolve my couch with my tears. My eye has wasted away with grief; It has become old because of all my adversaries." ~ Psalm 6:6-7

Why is it that we think God can't handle our emotions? After all, He created them. Many think it is awful to question why God does certain things.

God is never taken by surprise, nor is He shocked by anything we feel or question. In fact, Jesus told us life would be hard. *"Take up your cross,"* He said. *"They will mock you and persecute you because of me,"* He said.

It is ok for us to feel anger, anxiety, happiness, or sadness, and to question God when stinky things of life happen. **Where we err is when we stop trusting Him.**

If your children are feeling certain emotions, then that is a **great** time to turn them to prayer. In all circumstances, we should lead our kids to go to the Lord in prayer and tell Him every secret and burden.

Prepare to Pray!

Discuss with your children different types of events and the emotions they might feel. For example: winning a ballgame, losing a ballgame, feeling nervous before a performance, feeling anger toward a friend, bragging about a good grade, etc. Have them think about which type of emotion they might need help controlling. Are they worriers? Do they lose their tempers? Do they get depressed?

Use the scriptures in the back of this book to lead your child in prayer. If you have younger children, choose 1 or 2 verses to focus on depending upon the feelings they are dealing with. For older children, encourage them to choose a verse to memorize.

"For we do not have a high priest who cannot sympathize with our weaknesses, but One who has been tempted in all things as we are, yet without sin." ~ Hebrews 4:15

Children are growing in maturity and understanding. When young, they do not have a full grasp on human behavior and why people treat others the way they do.

Our kids can be hurt by others unintentionally or intentionally. Turning our children to prayer in such situations will help them to have their hearts healed by the High Priest who has been through as much as, or more than, they have.

How to Forgive Others Who Unintentionally Hurt Us

Has your child been excluded? Overlooked? Rejected? Dealt with unfairly? Or ignored? Many times, these actions happen without the knowledge of those who did the hurting. Accidents happen, and feelings can get hurt.

If this happens, we can lead our child in a prayer that admits the negative feelings toward the person who hurt them. Have your child ask the Lord for understanding and the power to not retaliate. Help him to ask for the forgiveness and mercy needed, and for wisdom to solve the issue, if needed.

How to Forgive Others Who Intentionally Hurt Us

When someone intentionally hurts us, that is called *persecution*. People who show our children no mercy, or who ridicule and hurtfully tease them, are purposefully attempting to wound them.

In these situations, it is important for us to remind our children that Jesus was ridiculed and persecuted until death. And if our kids are being persecuted because of their relationship with Jesus, then that is fulfillment of scripture.

Have your child pray for wisdom to know how to respond in love. Pray with your child. Ask for confirmation. Glorifying Jesus should be the motivation to respond in any situation. Take your time. Do not respond hastily. If the situation warrants it, contact your pastor or other adults that should be involved.

Bullying should not be tolerated. However, King Herod and Pilate sure did their share of bullying Jesus. And He remained silent through most of it.

On the cross He took the sins of Herod and Pilate upon Himself and then asked the Father to *"forgive them, for they know not what they do."*

We must exemplify the same forgiveness. Jesus does not ask us to do the easy thing. He asks us to do what glorifies the Father.

Prepare to Pray!

Use the scriptures in the back of this book to lead your child in prayer. If you have younger children, choose 1 or 2 verses to focus on. For older children, encourage them to choose a verse to memorize.

"And do not get drunk with wine, for that is dissipation, but be filled with the Spirit, speaking to one another in psalms and hymns and spiritual songs, singing and making melody with your heart to the Lord; always giving thanks for all things in the name of our Lord Jesus Christ to God, even the Father." ~ Ephesians 5:18-20

"But what about praying in one's prayer closet? Aren't we supposed to keep our prayers to ourselves? Isn't my relationship between only God and myself?"

Yes.

And no.

Just as there is a time for everything else in the world, there is a time for praying quietly and a time for praying aloud. There is a time for singing and dancing before the Lord, and a time to cease.

Prayer is **voicing** our needs and desires to the Father. Praise is **declaring** the wonders and great deeds of God. Petitioning is **asking** things of God.

See the pattern?

Why Pray Aloud?

I cannot stress enough how important it is to pray aloud with your children. For one thing, teaching them to pray aloud will help them listen to themselves. As we hear our own words, many times our hearts and attitudes will change.

Think of when you "talk out" or "rant" about a situation. Usually by the time you "get it out of your system," you are calm. Maybe you've figured out a solution, or you've realized you're wrong about something. The same thing happens when we "rant" to God.

If you haven't ever ranted aloud to God, then you should. It is so amazing how the Holy Spirit will guide your thoughts and attitudes because, really, we don't know how to pray for ourselves.

Why Have Kids Pray Aloud?

Attitudes towards praying aloud can be a spiritual thermometer. If your child regularly prays aloud, and then one day refuses to pray, that is a red flag; you can have a good spiritual discussion about what is going on.

The same goes for you. Are you willing to pray aloud? If not, search your heart for the reason why you won't.

Why Sing?

Scripture tells us to sing. We can sing praise, thanksgiving, and worship. I'm not saying you need to go join the choir. Some voices aren't made for that type of singing. Singing with the radio, or turning on gospel bluegrass on Sunday mornings, can put you into the worship mood!

Kids make up their own songs all the time. Encourage them to come up with their own worship songs. If music really isn't your thing, put the words of Bible verses to different rhythms while you're memorizing them. Not only does it help memorization, it is fun!

But What if I'm Too Shy to Sing or Pray Aloud?

I may ruffle feathers here, but I say . . . do the hard thing. Pray aloud anyway. I'm an introvert. I don't do well in front of crowds. I become very nervous. Just like anything else worth doing, praying out loud takes PRACTICE! The more you do it, the less nervous you will be.

I LOVE to pray aloud. Why? Because I'm talking to my Jesus, who saved me from the pit of hell. Shouldn't we be willing to pray in front of other people? Isn't the whole point of the gospel to spread it unto all nations? Others can't know the gospel unless we TELL it to them, and prayer is one way of doing that.

Think about it . . .

The enemy knows the power of prayer . . . so of course he wants you to be scared of praying in front of others. He wants you to think you won't say the "right" words. He will place any thoughts he can in your mind to squelch communication with your God.

I say to you, stop it!

Stop allowing the enemy to steal your prayer power!

Pray aloud!! SING!!! Even in your prayer closet! Be the one who steps up to pray for a meal in your house. Be the one to step up and pray on Sunday mornings at church. Be the one to whom people will defer for prayer when no one else in the room will pray aloud. BE the ONE who prays.

People will notice.

And so will your kids.

They will follow your lead.

Prepare to Pray!

Please practice praying out loud with your children. You will be absolutely amazed at how your spirits will entwine, and a sweet time of worship will take place. Insist on your children praying. You will not be disappointed.

Teaching Children to Pray During Times of Suffering, Abuse, or Death

"Keep me as the apple of the eye; Hide me in the shadow of Your wings; From the wicked who despoil me, My deadly enemies who surround me." ~ Psalm 17:8-9

**Preface – Suffering, abuse, and death are emotional and highly sensitive topics. I am no expert, but I do know my God. Also, if you EVER suspect abuse, please call the authorities. Thank you. ~ Anne Marie **

Suffering children can be found anywhere in the world. Walk into any local school and talk with the teachers; you will hear stories that break your heart. Children's ministry leaders deal with broken-hearted children as well. Those of us teaching Bible to kids deal with not only the hard problems, but the spiritual brokenness that comes through the hurt.

Children can suffer from:

- physical, mental, emotional, or sexual abuse;
- diseases such as childhood cancer and diabetes;
- neglect and malnutrition;
- effects of war;
- divorce;
- death of a parent or other family member; or
- rape.

Christian counseling is great. Medical assistance is a must. And we parents and leaders MUST prepare our children to **say *NO*** when in a situation that is uncomfortable, to **stand up for themselves** when someone tries to harm them, and to **run away** from harm to a safe adult, if possible.

Communication about Suffering, Abuse, or Death

If a child suffers trauma, we must communicate that he is **not** beyond redemption. Healing of all kinds can take place! They must understand that it is OK to feel sad and cry, but that they should not allow bitterness to take root in their hearts.

When scary images and thoughts threaten to take over their minds, we can encourage them to ask God to capture those thoughts and pictures and take them away.

Why Is There Suffering, Abuse, and Death?

The easy answer for why there is suffering, abuse, and death is because there is sin in the world. The complicated answer is . . . because there is sin in the world. Grief and sorrow have been a part of life ever since Adam and Eve made their choice in the garden. Adam and Eve had free will and chose to eat the fruit which allowed sinful behaviors.

People today still have that same free will, and people sometimes choose to hurt other people. It wasn't long until Adam and Eve had to deal with the death of their son and the fact that their other son was a murderer.

How Should We Pray Through Suffering, Abuse, or Death?

If you have a child who is suffering, be sure to talk about heaven! **There WILL be an end to all suffering.** There WILL be a time when people will not hurt other people. There WILL be a place where death does not exist!

Every person should be anticipating heaven and the return of Jesus. But those who deal with suffering are walking a road where desiring freedom from pain and suffering makes heaven more precious.

Why does God allow suffering? Because He loves us enough to give us free will. He allows us to either love Him or reject Him, to trust Him or not. But there is one truth we must have our children always remember: **ANYTHING bad that happens will turn out good in some way at the right time**.

Prepare to Pray!

Use the scriptures in the back of this book to lead your child in prayer. If you have younger children, choose 1 or 2 verses to focus on. For older children, encourage them to choose a verse to memorize.

"How can a young man keep his way pure? By keeping it according to Your word. With all my heart I have sought You; Do not let me wander from Your commandments." ~ Psalm 119:9-10

I love Psalm 119! It is full of verses that talk about loving God's commands, statutes, law, and precepts. Of course, all of those words mean the Bible.

If you and your children have worked your way through this book, then I commend you, and I'm sure you already have a quiet Bible time set aside.

Before Reading the Bible

Before reading the scriptures, encourage your kids to pray, asking God to give them **understanding** of the verses they are about to see. Have them pray that the Holy Spirit would help them to **focus** on the insights He will reveal.

Then have your children read for their quiet time. Even better, if they are situated in a prayer place, ask them to whisper the scripture out loud. That way they are seeing AND hearing the words. As the Holy Spirit works, He will cause the words to come alive and, at times, be sharper than a two-edged sword.

After Reading the Bible

If you have Bible reading at the same time, have everyone gather together at the end. Lead your children to pray that they will obey what they read and that the Holy Spirit will remind them of the scriptures when needed. Pray as a group until the habit is formed.

Encourage your children to read, pray, and read some more until God answers their prayers, or until they see a change in their situation.

God might even change their desires.

Prepare to Pray!

Use the scriptures in the back of this book to lead your child in prayer. If you have younger children, choose 1 or 2 verses to focus on. For older children, encourage them to choose a verse to memorize.

"'For I know the plans that I have for you,' declares the Lord, 'plans for welfare and not for calamity to give you a future and a hope.'" ~ Jeremiah 29:11

The future. It can be scary. It's the unknown. But we serve a mighty God who was the same yesterday as He is today, and He will be the same tomorrow. That should bring us hope.

And hope is what our kids need.

We live in a world where hopelessness reigns. People are tired and depressed; they seem to have no purpose. This is why it is important that our children know they have purpose with a Christian worldview, and that they serve a mighty King who cares about them. Our kids can be different than the world because they have HOPE!

Our kids can have hope in a future. That hope is not here on the earth—although that is part of it—but rather in a future that is eternal. This is a future that we need to share with others as we spread the gospel.

What to Pray for the Future

1. Pray for a clean heart. Psalm 51:10

2. Pray God's promises.

3. Forgiveness is huge. With forgiveness we can live a life in the fullness of joy and peace, knowing our personal worth in Christ.

4. Pray for a future spouse and family.

5. Pray to stay strong in the Lord when facing future temptations. Pray for the courage to run away from evil.

6. Have your child pray for guidance for how he will work in the kingdom. (Job, missionary, service, etc.)

7. Lead your children to pray for influence so that future souls will be won.

8. Thank God for a heavenly home.

Prepare to Pray!

Use the scriptures in the back of this book to lead your child in prayer. If you have younger children, choose 1 or 2 verses to focus on. For older children, encourage them to choose a verse to memorize.

SCRIPTURE CARDS

Tear out these pages, or cut them out. Cut apart the cards. Laminate them if you like. You can even use a hole punch to put holes in the upper left corner to put a ring through.

However you choose to use these cards, use them to help your children pray. Make copies if you have multiple children. Choose certain cards for certain situations.

It is OK if this book falls apart. Pray with your children and help them to become prayer warriors.

Verses to Help Us Pray
to the Father

The Father is Almighty:
For this reason also, God highly exalted Him, and bestowed on Him the name which is above every name, so that at the name of Jesus every knee will bow, of those who are in heaven and on earth and under the earth, and that every tongue will confess that Jesus Christ is Lord, to the glory of God the Father.
Philippians 2: 9-11

The Father is All-Seeing:
The eyes of the Lord are in every place, Watching the evil and the good.
Proverbs 15:3

The Father is All-Seeing:
O Lord, You have searched me and known me. You know when I sit down and when I rise up; You understand my thought from afar. You scrutinize my path and my lying down, And are intimately acquainted with all my ways. Even before there is a word on my tongue, Behold, O Lord, You know it all.
Psalms 139:1-4

The Father Has Unlimited Love:
For I am convinced that neither death, nor life, nor angels, nor principalities, nor things present, nor things to come, nor powers, nor height, nor depth, nor any other created thing, will be able to separate us from the love of God, which is in Christ Jesus our Lord.
Romans 8:38-39

The Father is Eternal:
Before the mountains were born Or You gave birth to the earth and the world, Even from everlasting to everlasting, You are God.
Psalm 90:2

The Father is Eternal:

Which He will bring about at the proper time—He who is the blessed and only Sovereign, the King of kings and Lord of lords, who alone possesses immortality and dwells in unapproachable light, whom no man has seen or can see. To Him be honor and eternal dominion! Amen.
1 Timothy 6:15-16

The Father Never Changes:

"For I, the Lord, do not change; therefore you, O sons of Jacob, are not consumed."
Malachi 3:6

The Father Never Changes:

Every good thing given and every perfect gift is from above, coming down from the Father of lights, with whom there is no variation or shifting shadow.
James 1:17

The Father is Our Abba:

For you have not received a spirit of slavery leading to fear again, but you have received a spirit of adoption as sons by which we cry out, "Abba! Father!"
Romans 8:15

The Father is Capable:

"I know that You can do all things, And that no purpose of Yours can be thwarted."
Job 42:2

The Father is Capable:

"Behold, I am the Lord, the God of all flesh; is anything too difficult for Me?"
Jeremiah 32:27

The Father is Everywhere:
Where can I go from Your Spirit? Or where can I flee from Your presence?
Psalm 139:7

The Father is Everywhere:
"Can a man hide himself in hiding places So I do not see him?" declares the Lord. "Do I not fill the heavens and the earth?" declares the Lord.
Jeremiah 23:24

Verses about

Forgiveness

Look upon my affliction and my trouble, And forgive all my sins.
Psalm 25:18

Help us, O God of our salvation, for the glory of Your name; And deliver us and forgive our sins for Your name's sake.
Psalm 79:9

For You, Lord, are good, and ready to forgive, And abundant in lovingkindness to all who call upon You.
Psalm 86:5

For if you forgive others for their transgressions, your heavenly Father will also forgive you. But if you do not forgive others, then your Father will not forgive your transgressions.
Matthew 6:14-15

Be kind to one another, tender-hearted, forgiving each other, just as God in Christ also has forgiven you.
Ephesians 4:32

If we confess our sins, He is faithful and righteous to forgive us our sins and to cleanse us from all unrighteousness.
1 John 1:9

70

Verses to help us pray
Anytime & Anywhere

Give ear to my words, O Lord, Consider my groaning. Heed the sound of my cry for help, my King and my God, For to You I pray. In the morning, O Lord, You will hear my voice; In the morning I will order my prayer to You and eagerly watch.
Psalm 5:1-3

The Lord has heard my supplication, The Lord receives my prayer.
Psalm 6:9

Blessed be God, Who has not turned away my prayer Nor His lovingkindness from me.
Psalm 66:20

But as for me, my prayer is to You, O Lord, at an acceptable time; O God, in the greatness of Your lovingkindness, Answer me with Your saving truth.
Psalm 69:13

With all prayer and petition pray at all times in the Spirit, and with this in view, be on the alert with all perseverance and petition for all the saints.
Ephesians 6:18

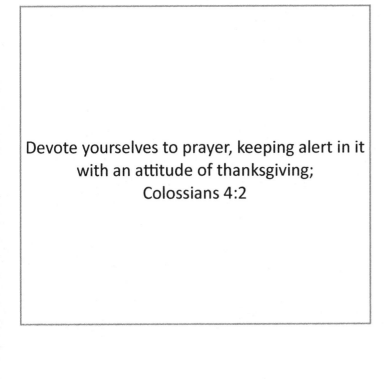

Devote yourselves to prayer, keeping alert in it
with an attitude of thanksgiving;
Colossians 4:2

Verses about
Praying about Big Things

Your faithfulness continues throughout all generations; You established the earth, and it stands.
Psalm 119:90

And they brought to Him a paralytic lying on a bed. Seeing their faith, Jesus said to the paralytic, "Take courage, son; your sins are forgiven."
Matthew 9:2

Then He touched their eyes, saying, "It shall be done to you according to your faith."
Matthew 9:29

Then Jesus said to her, "O woman, your faith is great; it shall be done for you as you wish." And her daughter was healed at once.
Matthew 15:28

"For nothing will be impossible with God."
Luke 1:37

But He said, "The things that are impossible with people are possible with God."
Luke 18:27

For we walk by faith, not by sight.
2 Corinthians 5:7

Having been buried with Him in baptism, in which you were also raised up with Him through faith in the working of God, who raised Him from the dead.
Colossians 2:12

Let no one look down on your youthfulness, but rather in speech, conduct, love, faith and purity, show yourself an example of those who believe.
1 Timothy 4:12

Now faith is the assurance of things hoped for, the conviction of things not seen.
Hebrews 11:1

By faith we understand that the worlds were prepared by the word of God, so that what is seen was not made out of things which are visible.
Hebrews 11:3

But he must ask in faith without any doubting, for the one who doubts is like the surf of the sea, driven and tossed by the wind.
James 1:6

Therefore, those also who suffer according to the will of God shall entrust their souls to a faithful Creator in doing what is right.
1 Peter 4:19

And without faith it is impossible to please Him, for he who comes to God must believe that He is and that He is a rewarder of those who seek Him.
Hebrews 11:6

Verses to Pray When
God Says "Not Yet"

Is anything too difficult for the Lord? At the appointed time I will return to you.
Genesis 18:14

"Take heed, keep on the alert; for you do not know when the appointed time will come."
Mark 13:33

But when the fullness of the time came, God sent forth His Son, born of a woman, born under the Law.
Galatians 4:4

And so, having patiently waited, he obtained the promise.
Hebrews 6:15

But do not let this one fact escape your notice, beloved, that with the Lord one day is like a thousand years, and a thousand years like one day.
2 Peter 3:8

Verses to Help Us Pray
Before an Event

Whoever speaks, is to do so as one who is speaking the utterances of God; whoever serves is to do so as one who is serving by the strength which God supplies; so that in all things God may be glorified through Jesus Christ, to whom belongs the glory and dominion forever and ever. Amen.
1 Peter 4:11

Keep the charge of the LORD your God, to walk in His ways, to keep His statutes, His commandments, His ordinances, and His testimonies, according to what is written in the Law of Moses, that you may succeed in all that you do and wherever you turn,
1 Kings 2:3

Therefore, confess your sins to one another, and pray for one another so that you may be healed. The effective prayer of a righteous man can accomplish much.
James 5:16

But the Helper, the Holy Spirit, whom the Father will send in My name, He will teach you all things, and bring to your remembrance all that I said to you.
John 14:26

Therefore, do not throw away your confidence, which has a great reward. For you have need of endurance, so that when you have done the will of God, you may receive what was promised.
Hebrews 10: 35-36

Verses to Help Us Pray
For Knowledge

I have filled him with the Spirit of God in wisdom, in understanding, in knowledge, and in all kinds of craftsmanship.
Exodus 31:3

"Give me now wisdom and knowledge, that I may go out and come in before this people, for who can rule this great people of Yours?"
2 Chronicles 1:10

"O our God, will You not judge them? For we are powerless before this great multitude who are coming against us; nor do we know what to do, but our eyes are on You."
2 Chronicles 20:12

Teach me good discernment and knowledge, For I believe in Your commandments.
Psalm 119:66

The fear of the Lord is the beginning of knowledge; Fools despise wisdom and instruction.
Proverbs 1:7

For the Lord gives wisdom; From His mouth come knowledge and understanding.
Proverbs 2:6

Every prudent man acts with knowledge, But a fool displays folly.
Proverbs 13:16

The mind of the prudent acquires knowledge, And the ear of the wise seeks knowledge.
Proverbs 18:15

As for these four youths, God gave them knowledge and intelligence in every branch of literature and wisdom; Daniel even understood all kinds of visions and dreams.
Daniel 1:17

"It is He who changes the times and the epochs; He removes kings and establishes kings; He gives wisdom to wise men And knowledge to men of understanding."
Daniel 2:21

To give to His people the knowledge of salvation By the forgiveness of their sins.
Luke 1:77

Because by the works of the Law no flesh will be justified in His sight; for through the Law comes the knowledge of sin.
Romans 3:20

Oh, the depth of the riches both of the wisdom and knowledge of God! How unsearchable are His judgments and unfathomable His ways!
Romans 11:33

But thanks be to God, who always leads us in triumph in Christ, and manifests through us the sweet aroma of the knowledge of Him in every place.
2 Corinthians 2:14

For God, who said, "Light shall shine out of darkness," is the One who has shone in our hearts to give the Light of the knowledge of the glory of God in the face of Christ.
2 Corinthians 4:6

Finally, brethren, whatever is true, whatever is honorable, whatever is right, whatever is pure, whatever is lovely, whatever is of good repute, if there is any excellence and if anything worthy of praise, dwell on these things.
Philippians 4:8

Verses to Help Us Pray
For World Events

Joshua then said to them, "Do not fear or be dismayed! Be strong and courageous, for thus the Lord will do to all your enemies with whom you fight."
Joshua 10:25

Put them in fear, O Lord; Let the nations know that they are but men.
Psalm 9:20

The fear of the Lord is clean, enduring forever; The judgments of the Lord are true; they are righteous altogether.
Psalm 19:9

Even though I walk through the valley of the shadow of death, I fear no evil, for You are with me; Your rod and Your staff, they comfort me.
Psalm 23:4

The Lord is my light and my salvation; Whom shall I fear? The Lord is the defense of my life; Whom shall I dread?
Psalm 27:1

Though a host encamp against me, My heart will not fear; Though war arise against me, In spite of this I shall be confident.
Psalm 27:3

Let all the earth fear the Lord; Let all the inhabitants of the world stand in awe of Him.
Psalm 33:8

I sought the Lord, and He answered me, And delivered me from all my fears.
Psalm 34:4

Therefore we will not fear, though the earth should change And though the mountains slip into the heart of the sea;
Psalm 46:2

The heavens are Yours, the earth also is Yours; The world and all it contains, You have founded them.
Psalm 89:11

Before the Lord, for He is coming, For He is coming to judge the earth. He will judge the world in righteousness And the peoples in His faithfulness.
Psalm 96:13

"For God so loved the world, that He gave His only begotten Son, that whoever believes in Him shall not perish, but have eternal life. For God did not send the Son into the world to judge the world, but that the world might be saved through Him. He who believes in Him is not judged; he who does not believe has been judged already, because he has not believed in the name of the only begotten Son of God. This is the judgment, that the Light has come into the world, and men loved the darkness rather than the Light, for their deeds were evil.
John 3:16-19

Then Jesus again spoke to them, saying, "I am the Light of the world; he who follows Me will not walk in the darkness, but will have the Light of life."
John 8:12

Verses to Help Us Pray

For Needy People

For the poor will never cease to be in the land; therefore I command you, saying, 'You shall freely open your hand to your brother, to your needy and poor in your land.'
Deuteronomy 15:11

"Because of the devastation of the afflicted, because of the groaning of the needy, Now I will arise," says the Lord; "I will set him in the safety for which he longs."
Psalm 12:5

I commend to you our sister Phoebe, who is a servant of the church which is at Cenchrea; that you receive her in the Lord in a manner worthy of the saints, and that you help her in whatever matter she may have need of you; for she herself has also been a helper of many, and of myself as well.
Romans 16:1-2

And my God will supply all your needs according to His riches in glory in Christ Jesus.
Philippians 4:19

Our people must also learn to engage in good deeds to meet pressing needs, so that they will not be unfruitful.
Titus 3:14

Therefore let us draw near with confidence to the throne of grace, so that we may receive mercy and find grace to help in time of need.
Hebrews 4:16

If a brother or sister is without clothing and in need of daily food, and one of you says to them, "Go in peace, be warmed and be filled," and yet you do not give them what is necessary for their body, what use is that?
James 2:15-16

But whoever has the world's goods, and sees his brother in need and closes his heart against him, how does the love of God abide in him?
1 John 3:17

Prayers for Change:

Deliverance

He said, "The Lord is my rock and my fortress and my deliverer."
2 Samuel 22:2

Since I am afflicted and needy, Let the Lord be mindful of me. You are my help and my deliverer; Do not delay, O my God.
Psalm 40:17

Deliver me from my enemies, O my God; Set me securely on high away from those who rise up against me.
Psalm 59:1

And I will give them one heart, and put a new spirit within them. And I will take the heart of stone out of their flesh and give them a heart of flesh.
Ezekiel 11:19

"You have heard that it was said, 'You shall love your neighbor and hate your enemy.' But I say to you, love your enemies and pray for those who persecute you, so that you may be sons of your Father who is in heaven; for He causes His sun to rise on the evil and the good, and sends rain on the righteous and the unrighteous. For if you love those who love you, what reward do you have? Do not even the tax collectors do the same? If you greet only your brothers, what more are you doing than others? Do not even the Gentiles do the same? Therefore you are to be perfect, as your heavenly Father is perfect. ~
Matthew 5:43-48

Let him know that he who turns a sinner from the error of his way will save his soul from death and will cover a multitude of sins.
James 5:20

O give us help against the adversary,
For deliverance by man is in vain.
Psalm 60:11

Prayers for Change:

Provision

Who covers the heavens with clouds, Who provides rain for the earth, Who makes grass to grow on the mountains.
Psalm 147:8

Isaac prayed to the Lord on behalf of his wife, because she was barren; and the
Lord answered him and Rebekah his wife conceived.
Genesis 25:21

"Indeed, forty years You provided for them in the wilderness and they were not in want;
Their clothes did not wear out, nor did their feet swell."
Nehemiah 9:21

Your creatures settled in it; You provided in Your goodness for the poor, O God.
Psalm 68:10

Prayers for Change:

Courage

"Be strong and courageous, do not be afraid or tremble at them, for the Lord your God is the one who goes with you. He will not fail you or forsake you."
Deuteronomy 31:6

Joshua then said to them, "Do not fear or be dismayed! Be strong and courageous, for thus the Lord will do to all your enemies with whom you fight."
Joshua 10:25

Wait for the Lord; Be strong and let your heart take courage; Yes, wait for the Lord.
Psalm 27:14

No temptation has overtaken you but such as is common to man; and God is faithful, who will not allow you to be tempted beyond what you are able, but with the temptation will provide the way of escape also, so that you will be able to endure it.
1 Corinthians 10:13

Open their eyes so that they may turn from darkness to light and from the dominion of Satan to God, that they may receive forgiveness of sins and an inheritance among those who have been sanctified by faith in Me.
Acts 26:18

Verses to Help Us Pray
Prayers of
Thanksgiving

Oh give thanks to the Lord, call upon His name; Make known His deeds among the peoples.
1 Chronicles 16:8

I shall wash my hands in innocence, And I will go about Your altar, O Lord, That I may proclaim with the voice of thanksgiving And declare all Your wonders.
Psalm 26:6-7

"He who offers a sacrifice of thanksgiving honors Me; And to him who orders his way aright I shall show the salvation of God."
Psalm 50:23

Let us come before His presence with thanksgiving, Let us shout joyfully to Him with psalms.
Psalm 95:2

Give thanks to the Lord, for He is good; For His lovingkindness is everlasting.
Psalm 118:1

Be anxious for nothing, but in everything by prayer and supplication with thanksgiving let your requests be made known to God.
Philippians 4:6

Devote yourselves to prayer, keeping alert in it with an attitude of thanksgiving;
Colossians 4:2

First of all, then, I urge that entreaties and prayers, petitions and thanksgivings, be made on behalf of all men,
1 Timothy 2:1

"Amen, blessing and glory and wisdom and thanksgiving and honor and power and might, be to our God forever and ever. Amen."
Revelation 7:12

Verses that Help Kids to Tell God How They Feel:

Questioning

"For My thoughts are not your thoughts, Nor are your ways My ways," declares the Lord. "For as the heavens are higher than the earth, So are My ways higher than your ways And My thoughts than your thoughts."
Isaiah 55:8-9

Now when John, while imprisoned, heard of the works of Christ, he sent word by his disciples and said to Him, "Are You the Expected One, or shall we look for someone else?"
Matthew 11:2-3

On the contrary, who are you, O man, who answers back to God? The thing molded will not say to the molder, "Why did you make me like this," will it?
Romans 9:20

Verses that Help Kids to Tell God How They Feel:

Worries or Concerns

When my anxious thoughts multiply within me, Your consolations delight my soul.
Psalm 94:19

Search me, O God, and know my heart; Try me and know my anxious thoughts;
Psalm 139:23

Say to those with anxious heart, "Take courage, fear not. Behold, your God will come with vengeance; The recompense of God will come, But He will save you."
Isaiah 35:4

'Do not fear, for I am with you; Do not anxiously look about you, for I am your God. I will strengthen you, surely I will help you, Surely I will uphold you with My righteous right hand.'
Isaiah 41:10

Be anxious for nothing, but in everything by prayer and supplication with thanksgiving let your requests be made known to God.
Philippians 4:6

Verses that Help Kids to Tell God How They Feel:

Anger

Then the Lord passed by in front of him and proclaimed, "The Lord, the Lord God, compassionate and gracious, slow to anger, and abounding in lovingkindness and truth;"
Exodus 34:6

And when he humbled himself, the anger of the Lord turned away from him, so as not to destroy him completely; and also conditions were good in Judah.
2 Chronicles 12:12

Do not hide Your face from me, Do not turn Your servant away in anger; You have been my help; Do not abandon me nor forsake me, O God of my salvation!
Psalm 27:9

Cease from anger and forsake wrath; Do not fret; it leads only to evildoing.
Psalm 37:8

He who is slow to anger has great understanding, But he who is quick-tempered exalts folly.
Proverbs 14:29

A gentle answer turns away wrath, But a harsh word stirs up anger.
Proverbs 15:1

A hot-tempered man stirs up strife, But the slow to anger calms a dispute.
Proverbs 15:18

Do not associate with a man given to anger; Or go with a hot-tempered man,
Proverbs 22:24

Now the deeds of the flesh are evident, which are: immorality, impurity, sensuality, idolatry, sorcery, enmities, strife, jealousy, outbursts of anger, disputes, dissensions, factions, envying, drunkenness, carousing, and things like these, of which I forewarn you, just as I have forewarned you, that those who practice such things will not inherit the kingdom of God.
Galatians 5:19-21

Verses that Help Kids to Tell God How They Feel:

Happiness

Then on the twenty-third day of the seventh month he sent the people to their tents, rejoicing and happy of heart because of the goodness that the Lord had shown to David and to Solomon and to His people Israel.
2 Chronicles 7:10

"Behold, how happy is the man whom God reproves, So do not despise the discipline of the Almighty."
Job 5:17

When you shall eat of the fruit of your hands, You will be happy and it will be well with you.
Psalm 128:2

She is a tree of life to those who take hold of her, And happy are all who hold her fast.
Proverbs 3:18

He who despises his neighbor sins, But happy is he who is gracious to the poor.
Proverbs 14:21

Where there is no vision, the people are unrestrained, But happy is he who keeps the law.
Proverbs 29:18

In the day of prosperity be happy, But in the day of adversity consider—God has made the one as well as the other So that man will not discover anything that will be after him.
Ecclesiastes 7:14

The faith which you have, have as your own conviction before God. Happy is he who does not condemn himself in what he approves.
Romans 14:22

Verses that Help Kids to Tell God How They Feel:

Sadness

Truly, truly, I say to you, that you will weep and lament, but the world will rejoice; you will grieve, but your grief will be turned into joy. Whenever a woman is in labor she has pain, because her hour has come; but when she gives birth to the child, she no longer remembers the anguish because of the joy that a child has been born into the world. Therefore you too have grief now; but I will see you again, and your heart will rejoice, and no one will take your joy away from you.
John 16:20-22

My soul has been rejected from peace; I have forgotten happiness.
Lamentations 3:17

My soul weeps because of grief; Strengthen me according to Your word.
Psalm 119:28

A joyful heart makes a cheerful face, But when the heart is sad, the spirit is broken.
Proverbs 15:13

126

Verses to Help Us

Forgive Others

"Blessed are those who have been persecuted for the sake of righteousness, for theirs is the kingdom of heaven. Blessed are you when people insult you and persecute you, and falsely say all kinds of evil against you because of Me."
Matthew 5: 10-11

But I say to you, love your enemies and pray for those who persecute you, so that you may be sons of your Father who is in heaven; for He causes His sun to rise on the evil and the good, and sends rain on the righteous and the unrighteous.
Matthew 5:44-45

For if you forgive others for their transgressions, your heavenly Father will also forgive you. But if you do not forgive others, then your Father will not forgive your transgressions.
Matthew 6:14-15

Whenever you stand praying, forgive, if you have anything against anyone, so that your Father who is in heaven will also forgive you your transgressions.
Mark 11:25

Who will separate us from the love of Christ? Will tribulation, or distress, or persecution, or famine, or nakedness, or peril, or sword?
Romans 8:35

And we toil, working with our own hands; when we are reviled, we bless; when we are persecuted, we endure;
1 Corinthians 4:12

Therefore I am well content with weaknesses, with insults, with distresses, with persecutions, with difficulties, for Christ's sake; for when I am weak, then I am strong.
2 Corinthians 12:10

130

Verses to Help Us
Pray Aloud &
Sing to God

Then Moses said, "I pray You, show me Your glory!"
Exodus 33:18

Then Hannah prayed and said, "My heart exults in the Lord; My horn is exalted in the Lord, My mouth speaks boldly against my enemies, Because I rejoice in Your salvation.
1 Samuel 2:1

I will give thanks to the Lord according to His righteousness And will sing praise to the name of the Lord Most High.
Psalm 7:17

I will give thanks to You, O Lord, among the peoples; I will sing praises to You among the nations.
Psalm 57:9

"And all things you ask in prayer, believing, you will receive."
Matthew 21:22

So they removed the stone. Then Jesus raised His eyes, and said, "Father, I thank You that You have heard Me."
John 11:41

But the Helper, the Holy Spirit, whom the Father will send in My name, He will teach you all things, and bring to your remembrance all that I said to you.
John 14:26

In the same way the Spirit also helps our weakness; for we do not know how to pray as we should, but the Spirit Himself intercedes for us with groanings too deep for words;
Romans 8:26

Verses to Help Us Pray Through

Suffering, Abuse,

& Death

The Lord said, "I have surely seen the affliction of My people who are in Egypt, and have given heed to their cry because of their taskmasters, for I am aware of their sufferings."
Exodus 3:7

Even though I walk through the valley of the shadow of death, I fear no evil, for You are with me; Your rod and Your staff, they comfort me.
Psalm 23:4

O Lord my God, I cried to You for help, and You healed me.
Psalm 30:2

Let those be ashamed and humiliated together Who seek my life to destroy it; Let those be turned back and dishonored Who delight in my hurt.
Psalm 40:14

For You have delivered my soul from death, Indeed my feet from stumbling, So that I may walk before God In the light of the living.
Psalm 56:13

God is to us a God of deliverances; And to God the Lord belong escapes from death.
Psalm 68:20

Precious in the sight of the Lord Is the death of His godly ones.
Psalm 116:15

But He was pierced through for our transgressions, He was crushed for our iniquities; The chastening for our well-being fell upon Him, And by His scourging we are healed.
Isaiah 53:5

Heal me, O Lord, and I will be healed; Save me and I will be saved, For You are my praise.
Jeremiah 17:14

The news about Him spread throughout all Syria; and they brought to Him all who were ill, those suffering with various diseases and pains, demoniacs, epileptics, paralytics; and He healed them.
Matthew 4:24

Those passing by were hurling abuse at Him, wagging their heads, and saying, "Ha! You who are going to destroy the temple and rebuild it in three days."
Mark 15:29

138

But when Jesus heard this, He said, "This sickness is not to end in death, but for the glory of God, so that the Son of God may be glorified by it."
John 11:4

For I consider that the sufferings of this present time are not worthy to be compared with the glory that is to be revealed to us.
Romans 8:18

But if we are afflicted, it is for your comfort and salvation; or if we are comforted, it is for your comfort, which is effective in the patient enduring of the same sufferings which we also suffer,
2 Corinthians 1:6

Being found in appearance as a man, He humbled Himself by becoming obedient to the point of death, even death on a cross.
Philippians 2:8

That I may know Him and the power of His resurrection and the fellowship of His sufferings, being conformed to His death;
Philippians 3:10

For indeed he was sick to the point of death, but God had mercy on him, and not on him only but also on me, so that I would not have sorrow upon sorrow.
Philippians 2:27

Now may our Lord Jesus Christ Himself and God our Father, who has loved us and given us eternal comfort and good hope by grace, comfort and strengthen your hearts in every good work and word.
2 Thessalonians 2:16-17

Therefore, confess your sins to one another, and pray for one another so that you may be healed. The effective prayer of a righteous man can accomplish much.
James 5:16

And He Himself bore our sins in His body on the cross, so that we might die to sin and live to righteousness; for by His wounds you were healed.
1 Peter 2:24

"And He will wipe away every tear from their eyes; and there will no longer be any death; there will no longer be any mourning, or crying, or pain; the first things have passed away."
Revelation 21:4

142

Verses to Help Us Pray for the

Future

As for you, O king, while on your bed your thoughts turned to what would take place in the future; and He who reveals mysteries has made known to you what will take place.
Daniel 2:29

Surely there is a future, And your hope will not be cut off.
Proverbs 23:18

Strength and dignity are her clothing, And she smiles at the future.
Proverbs 31:25

Instruct them to do good, to be rich in good works, to be generous and ready to share, storing up for themselves the treasure of a good foundation for the future, so that they may take hold of that which is life indeed. 1 Timothy 6:18-19

I have fought the good fight, I have finished the course, I have kept the faith; in the future there is laid up for me the crown of righteousness, which the Lord, the righteous Judge, will award to me on that day; and not only to me, but also to all who have loved His appearing.
2 Timothy 4:7-9

Dear Reader,

I hope this book has helped you form new habits with your children. Keep at it! **You are doing great things**.

Keep on keeping on!

Anne Marie Gosnell
FutureFlyingSaucers Resources

If this book helped you in any way, please consider leaving a review on Amazon, or the store where you purchased this.

And please tell your friends! When you tell your friends about FutureFlyingSaucers Resources then you help spread the gospel.

Made in the USA
Middletown, DE
13 August 2020

15071061R00084